Have Yourself An Eschatological Christmas

Christmas Hope in An Age of Pessimism

Have Yourself An Eschatological Christmas

Christmas Hope in An Age of Pessimism

JASON M. GARWOOD

Cross & Crown Books
Warrenton, VA

Have Yourself an Eschatological Christmas:
Christmas Hope in an Age of Pessimism

Copyright 2019 © Jason M. Garwood

Publisher:
Cross & Crown Books
41 West Lee Highway
Suite 59 Box #199
Warrenton, VA 20186

Cover Design: Red Bag Media

Scripture quotations taken from the New American Standard Bible® (NASB), Copyright © 1960, 1962, 1963, 1968, 1971, 1972, 1973, 1975, 1977, 1995 by The Lockman Foundation. Used by permission. www.Lockman.org

Printed in the United States of America.

ISBN-13: 978-1-7341228-1-7
ISBN-10: 1734122811

DEDICATION

To Gary North:
Whose war on entropy
is not forgotten.

CONTENTS

ACKNOWLEDGMENTS

Thank you, Holy Trinity, for showing up in history to give us hope for the future.

Thank you, Mary, for being an incredible wife. Thank you, Elijah, Avery, and Nathan, for bringing joy to me each day.

FOREWORD

There comes a time when you simply have to deal with the Bible and what it *actually says*, not what you think it says, or what you wished it would say. For a long time, my eschatological journey consisted of quoting dispensational authors and what *they* said about certain passages, and thus it didn't leave much room or time for biblical exegesis. I don't mean to suggest that pessimistic Christians and would be exegetes are making the *same* mistake, though I'm sure some of them are. For me, this was all I knew to do. Pentecost *this*, Moody *that*. Sprinkle in some Scofield study notes and *voila!* you now have a robust recipe for apocalypticism and Rapture doctrine. Or not.

While much could be said about my journey away from pessimillennialism, I'll spare those details for another book at another time (Lord willing). My present concern has everything to do with how we view Christmas, especially when we consider the nature and purpose of Christmas, not least how we view it in our age of rampant pessimism. We're going to spend some time thinking through the incarnation as it pertains to history, including, as it were, the future *of* history. Delving into such concepts as the intersection of the future and the past in the present will no doubt be some new territory for me. Connecting the Christmas story to what Christ came to do will be another tall order, especially when we deal with the eschatology inherent to it. The gospel of the Kingdom and its implications for history deserves our undivided attention and allegiance.

This small book is the product of a sermon series I preached and thus it has that sort of "feel" to it. One can only say what he can say in 40 minutes or less, and therefore I readily admit that much more work needs to go into a topic like this. I almost hate writing that. Here are you, the reader, coming to read and learn and I'm telling you that you'll probably have more work ahead of you. I sincerely apologize.

However, maybe that's a good thing; after all, if there's one thing I know about eschatology and history it is this: we have a long way to go. 'A long way to go', you ask?

I believe we're in the early church and I'm not the first to suggest this. Given the sheer magnitude of the promises found in the Old Testament (recapitulated and appropriated in the New Testament in light of Christ's coming), I believe we have quite a way to go to 'realize' that which Christ has 'inaugurated'. We haven't 'realized' the exegesis let alone the practice of eschatology in the here and now!

So, we have work to do. The Church is being inundated by the humanists who have taken over the henhouse, and it doesn't help that our pastors are bowing out of the fight. The pessimism being proclaimed from pulpits is deadening and dulling our soldiers and the culture around us is the resultant casualty. Ideas have consequences, and you can't beat something with nothing. If you don't have an answer to the problems, you don't have a 'something', which means, please stay with me, you have *nothing*. Lucky for you, we *do* have something in the Bible, and I'm here to tell you that it is *wonderful*.

Jason Garwood
Warrenton, VA
December 20, 2019

1

INCARNATIONAL DISCONTINUITY

In the beginning was the Word, and the Word was with
God, and the Word was God.
John 1:1

And the Word became flesh, and dwelt among us, and we
saw His glory, glory as of the only begotten from the
Father, full of grace and truth.
John 1:14

In the spirit of the song, "Have Yourself a Merry Little Christmas," I have chosen to hijack the moniker and call this book, "Have yourself an eschatological Christmas," mostly because I believe the Advent of Christ to be a worthy matter of discussion, especially during Advent Season. However, its significance, it seems to me, has dwindled in that we are oftentimes unable to see the true importance of the Word becoming flesh, largely because the Church does not have a grasp on the eschatological significance of the occasion. Our customary way of behaving is centered on many cultural items: Christmas trees, presents, food, and family. These things in and of themselves are not *innately* pagan or problematic. (I repeat!) They can be stewarded to the glory of God because it's not what goes into a man that defiles him, but what comes out from his heart that taints him and renders him unclean (Matt. 15:11).

Nevertheless, I do believe that the greater threat to our understanding of Christmas is *not* Christmas trees, cookies, and a decorated house. The greatest threat to our understanding of Christmas is pietism exacerbated by pessimism. It is the pietist who lacks an ethical/judicial hermeneutic for Christmas. It is the pietist who sees culture as being an enemy rather than something to be cultivated and propogated. It is the pietist whose pessimism is perpetuated in our churches—to give you an alliteration. And what is the pessimism I'm addressing? The doctrinal demeanor that suggests that Christ's incarnation has nothing to do with history, and that our history is headed towards abject failure and inexorable disaster. This historical, entropic pessimism has led to retreatism and a fully conscious surrender of the world into the hands of evil.

Whenever pessimism towards present circumstances and future prospects runs its course, dominating Christian thinking and philosophy, we would be wise to respond by figuring out where it came from. When we have a pessimistic outlook, we need to ask some questions: What are we supposing about the fall of Adam? What is it about Adam's sin that is so pervasive that even the resurrection of Christ is unable to rectify the damage? Or, has Christ's resurrection upended the sinful devastation incurred by Adam and Eve? If so, how? In what ways can we speak of the incarnation of Christ as it relates to real, historical progress? That's what I intend to answer in this book.

When speaking of eschatology, it's important for us to keep in mind that we are not speaking primarily about the end of the space/time universe. It is a narrow-minded view which suggests that, when talking about eschatology, we're dealing with the Second Coming of Christ *only*. To the contrary, eschatology ought to be defined as that system of theology that seeks to understand how the future intersects with both the past and the present. We're not navel-gazing Rapture aficionados who are completely inept at seeing the connection between Christ's incarnation, death, resurrection, and the progress of the gospel in history. Eschatology is not about charts and speculation and hand wringing nervousness. Eschatology, banking on the authority of Christ's present session as Leader and Savior (Acts 5:31), seeks to learn the significance of the gospel of the Kingdom as it navigates the halls of history and the road to the future. In short: eschatology is the study of gospel hope as it blazes a trail into the glorious, Kingdom future. Or perhaps more apt to what I intend to discuss in this chapter: *Eschatology is the study of the glorious Kingdom future as it blazes a trail into the present.*

The reason I criticize our woefully mislead dispensational brothers and sisters is because of this principle, which has been well established by folks in our movement: *Christians believe in God, but not history. Humanists believe in history, but not God.* Humanists, who desire to transcend themselves through the vehicle of radical, atheistic, Statist experimentation, believe a lot in history as it moves forward into a communist sunset. Christians, who believe in the gospel of Jesus Christ, desire to *escape* history, believing that a rapturous sunset is far more glorious than the hard work of establishing the kingdom of God in every institution of life. We'll come back to these ideas in the chapters ahead.

The title of this first chapter is called "Incarnational Discontinuity," and I'll tell what you I mean by this in a moment.

John 1:1 declares the truth about Jesus the Christ: "In the beginning was the Word, and the Word was with God, and the Word was God." Jesus the Speech of God was in the beginning, which ought to be understood in relation to Genesis 1:1, "In the beginning God created the heavens and the earth." The "beginning," which is a timestamp referencing the very start of the created order, is what John has in mind when he describes the 'origins' of Lord Jesus. The Word of God was there in the very beginning. Before things were created, Jesus was there, *uncreated*. He was 'with' God, himself being a part of the Triune Godhead, and thus the Word was God. We are not talking about the distant god of deism, nor are we talking about a pantheistic monism—this inchoate, vague god yet to be developed (we just need more time and more carbon taxes). Jesus is the Word, the Word is a part of the Godhead, thus he is God himself.

On top of this, the remarkable thing that John tells us in verse 14 is this: "And the Word became flesh and lived among us, and we have seen his glory, the glory as of a father's only son, full of grace and truth." The exceptional thing about Christmas (and I use that word interchangeably with the advent/incarnation of Christ), is the fact that *it was the ultimate historical disruption.* History had been *continuously* marked by sin and flailing covenantal conformity to the law covenant *outside* of man; however, the incarnation, being a strange and unusual event in history, was in fact the great *discontinuity* of all of history.

I repeat, with further emphasis: Jesus the Word taking on human flesh is one of two great acts of discontinuity in history, the other being is his resurrection (which we'll get to in chapter 3). *The incarnation of Christ was not a mystical event leading to a religion of mysticism, it was an ethical event which birthed a religion of dominion.* The incarnation can rightly be called an ethical event based on the fact that what Christ had done by taking on flesh was disrupt the stronghold of Satan, sin, and death by restoring man through the power of regeneration. This was done not by the snap of a finger, but by the Spirit's implantation of the law of God within the hearts of God's covenantally faithful people throughout history, causing them to walk in his ways with the end goal of Christianizing the world (cf. Ezekiel 36:22ff).

One of the things we need to consider is the intersection of the past, present, and future as it pertains to our experience of time in history. This is no small task, and plenty of ink has been spilled in the process. Nevertheless, I believe if we can get a few principles down, we can begin to think rightly about time and history and gospel optimism. I want to start by quoting R.J. Rushdoony from his book *Revolt Against Maturity*:

> On the one hand, the days, times present, are evil; on the other hand, these days must be eagerly redeemed as a season of great value and meaning. The contrast is a dramatic one. Instead of flight from evil days, there is an eager purchase or redemption of them as a time or season of great profit and advantage under God....For this reason, because the godly man's concern is to redeem the time, Christians, and especially Puritans, have been highly conscious of time and the clock. As a valuable commodity, time cannot be wasted. This horror of wasting time is alien to those outside the world of Biblical faith. Consciousness of time is for the ungodly a consciousness of decay and death, and drunkenness

and a sick gaiety are sought as escapes from that awareness.[1]

All men experience time, and for the regenerate Christian, time is a blessing to be redeemed. It has "great value and meaning." Why? Because under God we can work towards the advancement of Christian civilization without being a 'slave' to time. We don't need to *escape* time; we need to *redeem* time. Time isn't something to fear, it's something to embrace, something to redeem for the purposes of God and his Kingdom. The incarnation of Christ did not have the goal of redeeming man *from* space and time, but instead to redeem man from ethical deviation for the *purposes* of space and time.

Dispensationalists and other pietistic Christians don't have a fully developed category for understanding time, and thus, eschatology. But Christians have always been thoughtful about time, especially the Puritans. Harold Berman gives an apt description of the issue:

> In contrast to the other Indo-European peoples, including the Greeks, who believed that time moved in ever recurring cycles, the Hebrew people

[1] Rousas John Rushdoony, *Revolt against Maturity: A Biblical Psychology of Man* (Vallecito, CA: Ross House Books, 1987), 230.

conceived of a time as continuous, irreversible, and historical, leading to ultimate redemption at the end. They also believed, however, that time has periods within it. It is not cyclical but may be interrupted or accelerated. It develops. The Old Testament is a story not merely of chance but of development, of growth, of movement toward the messianic age—very uneven movement, to be sure, with much backsliding but nevertheless a movement *toward*. Christianity, however, added an important element the Judaic concept of time: that of transformation of the old into the new. The Hebrew Bible became the Old Testament, its meaning transformed by its fulfillment in the New Testament. In the story of the Resurrection, death was transformed into a new beginning. The times were not only accelerated but regenerated. This introduced a new structure of history, in which there was a fundamental transformation of one age into another. This transformation, it was believed, could only happen once: the life, death, and resurrection of Christ was thought to be the only major interruption in the course of linear time from the creation of the world until it ends altogether.[2]

---

[2] Harold J. Berman, *Law and Revolution: The Formation of the Western Legal Tradition* (Cambridge, Massachusetts: Harvard University Press, 1983), pp. 26-27. Quoted in Gary North, *Is the World Running Down?* (Tyler, Texas: Institute for Christian Economics, 1988), pp. 148-149.

Having said that, I think it's important to consider the concepts of past, present, and future. This is largely misunderstood, and given what I have already said, you can see why the dominion religion is rejected in favor of either the power religion, or the escapist religion. So, what is the past? What is the present? And what is the future? Because the future just met us in this present, and now it's already past—even right this very moment—what are we to think of this?

The only way to comprehend time is by using a mathematical formulation, usually referred to as a 'timeline'. On this line we have a dot which we can label, 'present'. The left side of the line is the 'past', while the right side is the 'future'. The intersection of the future with the past is in the present. Which means we can narrow our understanding of the present down to this: 1) The present is the beginning and the end of the times of past and future. It links and distinguishes between the two. 2) The present is always the *simultaneity* of past and future. The future is *always* flowing into the present and then filtered out the back into the past.

The unique thing about our experience of time lies in the fact that the past is always remembered, and the future is always something we hope for.

Consider this thought: if the future gives us past, which it does, and yet the past cannot give us future, then it follows that the future has a certain superiority and priority over everything else. If it's true that time is irreversible (we can't go back in time, though it does make for a fascinating science-fiction movie), then it follows that the *source* of time is always in the future. Time only comes to us from the future.

My point in bringing this up lies in the fact that the incarnation, which happened 2,000 years ago, did something more than just disrupt history for a few first century Jews in Palestine. The incarnation of Christ wasn't just a one-off event, an anomaly in an otherwise random universe of chaos and disorder naturalist progression. *The incarnation of the Word was a time-changing moment of history-altering hope.*

Revelation 5 intimates that history is rolled up like a scroll, and this is because of the fact that God not only sits enthroned over and beyond time but *enters into time with his whole being.* The Lamb worthy to break the scroll is the same Lamb who was born, died, and was raised. God isn't simply 'above time', he is authoritatively the sovereign *judge* of time. Time happens because God *is*. The incarnation was the discontinuous moment when the judge stepped into the room called time.

We know the future of Christ's already established Kingdom is bright. Christians will largely agree that. Despite the details of the end of history, Christ will be triumphant. But what many Christians fail to understand is the fact that the incarnation of Christ was the future coming into the present (now past). Let me repeat what I said earlier: *Eschatology is the study of the glorious Kingdom future as it blazes a trail into the present.* When the Word became flesh, the future came bursting forth on the scene of history. It wasn't as though God had to catch up to history and send his son. Rather, the son is *already* future, and he came into the present (now past) in order to bring the blessings of this glorious future to bear in the here and now.

The key concept here has to do with the significance of Christ's advent. This is not a momentary interruption, a pesky boulder in the middle of the river of time which breaches the smooth current of water downstream. Interruptions happen all every single day. A car accident interrupts your day, but a week later, things are basically back to normal (assuming no one died, which is a larger eschatological interruption, which we'll get to in a couple chapters). A flat tire, a long line, an unforeseen expense—these are interruptions that 'come our way'. They happen to us for various reasons. The future rushes into the present and it alters our course, but only slightly. Afterwards things usually go back to normal.

The incarnation was not that. The reason the incarnation can't been seen as a momentary interruption in history is because of what the incarnation gives us: *regeneration.* And regeneration isn't simply a drug injected in the arm for a slight and momentary 'high'. Regeneration changes everything because regeneration comes not just from the future, it comes from the God of the future.

When a man is converted, everything is changed. It is a life-altering situation. His habits change. His affections change. His priorities change. Everything is now different. The New Birth that the Spirit gives to us—the Spirit being a deposit given for future promises—is now a brand-new way to experience reality: space and time included. Future glory is now made tangible. We get a foretaste of the glory. The implication? *We live for the future rather than trying to escape from it.* Mere interruption in day-to-day life will only disturb you for a season. Regeneration? It changes your life; and it changes *history.*

This is why the incarnation ought to be seen as a discontinuous act of God. The Word made flesh is a time-altering, world-changing event which sets the course for a new future, and thus a new history. Because the Word became flesh and dwelt among us, we are now in a position to purchase more time for more dominion projects. This is the precious nature of the gospel promise.

And in response, what we must *not* do is complain about time. We must *redeem* time. We must buy it back from the banks of heaven. And the way we buy it is through ethical obedience. We do not buy time with the currency of unfaithfulness; we buy time through conformity to Christ and his law-word.

So, by all means, have yourself an eschatological Christmas. But do so knowing that the great discontinuity of the virgin-born child isn't just something we remember; it's something we possess for the advancement of the Kingdom in history. God demonstrated his control *over* history by his victory *inside* of history, and that demonstration is an ongoing project that involves every single one of us.

May Christ the King be honored in this nation and in this world!

2
ESCHATOLOGICAL POLITICS

For a child will be born to us, a son will be given to us;
And the government will rest on His shoulders; And His
name will be called Wonderful Counselor, Mighty God,
Eternal Father, Prince of Peace. There will be no end to the
increase of His government or of peace, On the throne of
David and over his kingdom, To establish it and to uphold
it with justice and righteousness from then on and
forevermore. The zeal of the LORD of hosts will
accomplish this.
Isaiah 9:6-7

In the previous chapter we established a few principles, and I want to simply remind you of what we said, because I intend to build on them as we go.

First: Pietism has resulted in pessimism which has led the Church to a fully conscious surrender of the world into the hands of evil. Ideas have consequences and bad ideas have *really* bad consequences.

Second: Eschatology is the study of the glorious Kingdom future as it blazes a trail into the present. Eschatology isn't primarily about speculation of the future history; it's about the future *of* history itself. It's taking what has been already established in our past, namely the gospel of Jesus Christ, and seeing how it works itself out as history rushes forward into the Kingdom sunset. (This will be our main focus.)

Third: By and large, Christians believe in God but not history, while humanists believe in history, but not God. Pietism/Eastern Mysticism and Western materialism are both really bad ditches to end up in.

Fourth: The incarnation of Christ was not a mystical event leading to a religion of mysticism, it was an ethical event which birthed a religion of dominion. This is incredibly important to grasp, especially if we are to take seriously what Jesus has told us, and not what we *think* he has told us.

Fifth: The incarnation of Christ did not have the goal of redeeming man *from* space and time, but instead to redeem man from ethical deviation for the *purposes* of space and time. Again, it is assumed from the New Testament that a regenerated person has now been brought into the Kingdom for the purpose of taking those Kingdom principles into the rest of the world. We were bought with a price, therefore, glorify God in your bodies, not just your metaphysical meanderings.

Let's consider our text. In Isaiah 9, we have the *locus classicus* of all passages pertaining to the birth of Jesus Christ. We are told in the first part of the chapter that there is gloom and anguish in Israel, but this will be no more (vs. 1). What is he talking about? Isaiah ministered during the time of King Ahaz, and more importantly, he ministered during the time of Assyria's impending invasion. In fact, history shows that Assyria would eventually destroy Damascus, the capital of Syria, and then would march on Israel, the Northern Kingdom of that time, and destroy Samaria, its capital city. In 722 B.C. this prophetic word came true: Israel was defeated, and many people were displaced and dispersed—the ultimate exile.

Judah, which was the Southern Kingdom of the former Israelite monarchy, was also at risk of invasion because of her haughtiness. (Keep in mind that Israel as a whole had more bad kings than good ones!) During Isaiah's ministry, however, Judah's judgment was put on hold, only because of the patience and long-suffering of God. But not for long. Two hundred years later, in 586 B.C., Babylon would destroy her and sack the capital city of

Jerusalem, the city of David, forcing them into exile as well.

At the end of Isaiah 8, we see that light—the illumination of the Holy Spirit's word—has dwindled (vs. 20). They have no "dawn." Due to their flagrant covenantal apostasy, people are going to be distressed and hungry (vs. 21). These covenant-abandoning people don't want the lamp of God's word to be a light unto their path; they would much rather go their own way. *Such is the obstinate person.* In verse 22 they look to the earth for hope rather than the teaching and testimony of the law of God. In view of that fact, they reap what they sow: distress and darkness, "the gloom of anguish," and thus they are driven into darkness.

The first part of Isaiah 9 is God's future-to-them plan to bring about "a great light" (v. 2) in order to restore God's people for the great purpose of establishing the kingdom of God on earth as it is in heaven. Unbelieving Israel, and unbelieving Gentiles, too, will see this light and both Matthew and Luke quote this verse as being fulfilled in the birth of Jesus Christ. He is light coming into the world. He is the teaching and the testimony made flesh. Quite literally, then, we can conclude that *Christmas is God's invasion plan.* The God who created the womb has now entered the womb. What Adam had done, Messiah's coming has now undone. The darkness that had befallen the wayward people would be chased away by the arrival of the child.

"For to us a child has been born." The answer to sin and darkness is the birth of a child, but not just any child, the *Christ* child. The coming child of the promise, what we call 'Christmas' is God's assertion of sovereignty and authority over the domain of darkness. Islam says that God cannot possibly have a son. Yet, Christianity teaches something altogether different: God *does* have a son. And what sort of God bothers with sending a son? The sort of God who is sovereign, who has unending authority; the one who alone has evil on a tightly woven, decidedly short, leash. The sort of God who knows that only through his son's actions in history can there be found a fresh and efficacious solution to the plight of man. If Isaiah teaches us anything here as it pertains to Christmas it is this: Salvation doesn't come *from* the earth, it comes *to* the earth. The world falls underneath the authority and jurisdiction of the Triune God, and so God *acts*. Evil's leash— controlled by God's sovereignty—is actually a noose. In Christ, God strangles death to death.

It's important to know, therefore, that *Christmas*

is a military operation. Isaiah 42:13 says that God is a man of war. What do I mean by this? In verse 6 Isaiah tells us that "the government will rest on his shoulders." What is Isaiah getting at? I take this to mean that the rule and reign of God will be placed solely on the shoulders of Jesus Christ. He is Messiah the Prince, which means he has full, legislative authority. He has Kingdom authority. The rule and reign of Christ will be placed on this child. We need to take seriously what the text says, not what we wished it would say. This 'child', Isaiah tells us, will have the rule and reign of God placed on his shoulders. (Which, by the way, is why Herod had a 'freak out' moment when he was informed of the birth of the new King.)

When the child is born, he would, like strapping on a backpack, come and carry with him the kingdom of heaven on the earth. In other words, *Christ's mediatorial reign began at his birth.* Don't miss this, because dispensationalists and other pessimistic Christians miss it. Christ's kingdom was given to him at his birth. He doesn't come back to the earth a second time to get a millennial kingdom. He already possesses it! *Christ's Kingdom was given to him at his birth, legally actualized in his death and resurrection, and asserted in the world at his ascension.* Which means that Christ's kingdom is not an adjunct, an add-on, to the kingdoms of men. The world boasts in centralized planning, administrative law, and bureaucratic red tape. Our boast is Christ: we have a child! His rule and reign is comprehensive, touching every person and intuition—*nothing* is off limits.

The tremendous burden of the kingdom of heaven was put on this child, which means that when he comes, the Kingdom comes; and when this takes place, Isaiah insists, the powers and principalities will be *toppled*. Why do I know this? Because Isaiah 9:7 *tells* us as much.

"There will be no end to the increase of his government or of peace." The rule and reign of the kingdom of heaven placed on his shoulders will grow. It will 'increase', which is to say, it will multiply greatly—that's simply the nature of the Kingdom. It has no place for stunted growth or regression, and this growth is a feature to the operation. As a son of David, he sits on David's throne "over his kingdom, to establish it and to uphold it with justice and righteousness from then on and forevermore." From *when* on? From 'then' on, as in, *from the day that child comes into their future.*

25

At this point, the question for us is this: Was Jesus self-conscious about Isaiah's expectation? When we read the Gospels, are we confronted with a man who knew the eschatological politics of what he was doing, or did Jesus not understand the times? More to the point: did Jesus believe his preaching to constitute an impending, history changing, eschatological event? If so, what *was* that event? Why was that event meaningful?

Questions such as these have been discussed by men in recent past and I will only mention one because I don't want to go too far down the rabbit trail. At the turn of the twentieth century, Albert Schweitzer had decided to go back into the world of the New Testament in order to trace the historical Jesus. (Heads up: anytime you hear someone say, "Historical Jesus," you are likely to be encountering someone who is about to deploy atheistic/pagan presuppositions.)

Schweitzer's quest was simple: get rid of the Jesus of faith in order to discover the true man, Jesus of Nazareth, and thus bring an end to the Church's control of Jesus. He concluded several things, and I would refer you to some of the writings of N.T. Wright and Jürgen Moltmann for further study.

What Schweitzer decided was that Jesus of

Nazareth was a product of the first century environment of apocalypticism. There were many end-of-the-world type messianic movements before Jesus, and plenty after, and Jesus was just one man in the line of other doomsday prophets ushering in the next revolution. So he argued.

The line of reasoning goes as follows: 1) Jesus thought the end was near, so he sent his disciples off on a mission to preach the good news of the Kingdom. The problem? *They came back.* There was no grand apocalyptic end. 2) Jesus decides to hasten the end of time by causing problems in Jerusalem, thus incurring the wrath of Rome and dying on a cross. Again, no ginormous end to the space/time continuum. Israel was still under Roman occupation. There was no apocalyptic deliverance. 3) After the second failed attempt at ushering in the apocalyptic kingdom, the disciples, after the Easter 'appearances' of Jesus, took Jesus from the realm of eschatology and apocalypticism, and brought him into the Church under the guise of ecclesiastical sacerdotalism. To sum it up: Jesus was wrong about what he was saying, therefore, any moral profundity we can conjure up will have to be done apart from Jesus, and certainly apart from his Spirit working in us.

You might be asking why I would bring this up. The reason I bring Schweitzer into this discussion is because, like Schweitzer, *we have pessimistic Christians who draw eerily similar conclusions as he did.* I'm sure you've heard the arguments: "Jesus didn't really bring the Kingdom." "Jesus was wrong in the Olivet Discourse about the generation passing away and the end coming." "Jesus said nothing about the kingdom of God coming to the earth because that's only going to happen in the future millennial reign when he sits on David's literal throne in literal Jerusalem after a third literal temple is literally constructed. *Literally.*" More could be said, but I'll spare you.

To the contrary, Jesus told us a lot about the imminent coming of the Kingdom. He preached the gospel of God in Galilee, saying, "The time is fulfilled, and the kingdom of God is at hand; repent and believe in the gospel" (Mk. 1:14-15). He instructed the religious leaders: "If I cast out demons by the Spirit of God, then the kingdom of God has come upon you" (Matt. 12:28). John the Baptist, discerning the times, said, "Repent, for the kingdom of heaven is at hand" (Matt. 3:2).

We were told to pray, "Your kingdom come, your will be done, on earth as it is in heaven" (Matt.

6:10). In Matthew 13 we learn of several parables describing the growing nature of the Kingdom as Jesus describes his present ministry's intentions. My contention? *Jesus absolutely understood what Isaiah had said about him.* The Kingdom is on his shoulders: It is his responsibility, and there will be no end to its increase. Jesus also told his disciples in Luke 12:32, "Do not be afraid, little flock, for your Father has chosen gladly to give you the kingdom."

Who could forget the powerful statement of Jesus in John 3:3, "Truly, truly, I say to you, unless one is born again he cannot see the kingdom of God." This is very straightforward: no regeneration, no Kingdom. No repentance, no regeneration. Only by being born again can one see and enter and participate in the Kingdom. And lastly, what does the apostle Paul say in Colossians 1:13? "For he rescued us from the domain of darkness and transferred us to the kingdom of his beloved son."

When speaking of the self-consciousness of Jesus' own understanding of himself and his ministry, no doubt Jesus knew of Daniel 7:13-14, "I kept looking in the night visions, and behold, with the clouds of heaven, one like a Son of Man was coming, and he came up to the Ancient of Days, and was presented before Him. And to him was given dominion, glory, and a kingdom, that all the peoples, nations and men of every language might serve him. His dominion is an everlasting dominion which will not pass away; and his kingdom is one which will not be destroyed."

Jesus would often refer to himself as 'son of man', which is both a self-conscious description from this passage, and passages in Ezekiel who was also called a 'son of man'. As the perfect human being, this son of man was faithful in discharging his responsibilities before the Father, and thus, in his death, resurrection, and ascension, *the Kingdom was asserted and unleashed in the world*. Jesus knew the texts: he enacted the will of the Father in obedience to the law of God, and God granted him the nations as his inheritance (Ps. 2:8).

In the world of eschatology, there are several misunderstandings when it comes to the now-present Kingdom and its implications for the world. The debate surrounds the language of 'already' and 'not yet'. As postmillennialists, we believe that the Kingdom is 'already' here in the world and 'not yet' *consummated*. This is because the Kingdom, which started as a rock that entered into the first century to destroy the kingdom of Rome, will gradually grow to become a mountain that fills the whole earth (see

Daniel 2:35; cf. 2:44-45).

What we *don't* mean is the schizophrenic, "The Kingdom is 'already' here, but 'not really' here yet." Or worse, "The Kingdom came *spiritually* 'already,' but it's 'not yet' here physically"—as if Neoplatonism has offered anything good to mankind. We also don't want to delve into hermeneutical gymnastics by saying, "The Kingdom is established in heaven 'already,' however, it is 'not yet' established on earth, and won't be until Jesus comes and sets up his earthly reign."

The reason I'm calling this chapter 'Eschatological Politics' is because the process for the restoration of all things—what we call the 'new heavens' and 'new earth'—has *already begun* and it touches on every area of life because in the birth of Christ the government of the Kingdom was placed on his shoulders. The great responsibility of gathering a fully regenerated, covenantally faithful people for the purposes of transforming all nations and institutions began the moment Christ entered the womb. The political interests of God on the earth started the moment the Holy Spirit conceived the miraculous unification of the divine Son of God with humanity in the womb of the virgin.

The process has 'already' begun. The Kingdom is

'already' here, and 'already' growing by leaps and bounds. Jesus' preaching which included an impending, history changing, eschatological event, was the old heavens and old earth passing away—what we call the old covenant—and the subsequent transformation of the old into a new creation, the coming of the new heavens and the new earth (more in chapter 4). This was established definitively and principally in his death, resurrection, and ascension. The Christ event—his death and resurrection and ascension—was the impending, history changing, eschatological event. It was the great legislative moment when God asserted his political vision for the cosmos.

Which means that *our cosmology is only properly understood when we grasp the political significance of the Christ child's shoulder-bearing government for the rest of history.* Christ has called all men, women, and children to come to him for forgiveness. He has demanded the unconditional surrender of the world. King Jesus desires the magistrate to repent, believe the gospel, and seek to uphold justice for the poor. King Jesus desires families to come to him to be healed for proper function for the health of all other spheres and institutions. He desires the Church to develop a politic of social action based on this remarkable event in history for the advancement of the Kingdom.

If it's true that the Kingdom that Christ proclaimed is synonymous with the new covenant he established in his blood—and it is—then it follows that the current Christian status quo is severely handicapped. We have memorialized Christmas while rejecting the political implications of it. We have opted for a safe Christianity instead of one that dares to press the crown rights of King Jesus into every area of life. May it never be!

Our task is to take what we get in the Christmas story, which is, as I have argued, a comprehensive salvation for comprehensive restoration of all men and social institutions and *do* something with it. Don't memorialize the Christmas story, *act* on it. Don't just celebrate the birth of Christ, *deal* with the what the birth of Christ truly means for you and the rest of the world....*healing.*

3
FIRST FRUITS OF THE PRESENT FUTURE

*But now Christ has been raised from the dead, the first
fruits of those who are asleep. For since by a man came
death, by a man also came the resurrection of the dead. For
as in Adam all die, so also in Christ all will be made alive.
But each in his own order:* **Christ the first fruits, after that
those who are Christ's at His coming, then comes the end,
when He hands over the kingdom to the God and Father,
when He has abolished all rule and all authority and power.**
*For He must reign until He has put all His enemies under
His feet. The last enemy that will be abolished is death. For
He has put all things in subjection under His feet. But when
He says, "All things are put in subjection," it is evident that
He is excepted who put all things in subjection to Him.
When all things are subjected to Him, then the Son Himself
also will be subjected to the One who subjected all things to
Him, so that God may be all in all.*
1 Corinthians 15:20-28

We are going to focus our attention on verses
23-24 of this passage and in a little while I'm going
to appeal to some other Scriptures to make sure we

understand what it is the Bible is getting at as it pertains to the ministry of Jesus, specifically his resurrection. At this point in our study, I have been focusing on the significance of the birth of Christ, however, as has been rather self-evident, we cannot take the birth of Christ and sever it from the rest of what Christ has come to do. The birth of Christ led to the life of Christ which led to death of Christ, which then gave way to the resurrection of Christ and the subsequent ascension of Christ. We can, in a matter of speaking, emphasize the different aspects of Jesus all the while keeping in mind that we aren't to be reductionists who separate those things out, pitting them against one another. They are separate pieces but they're the type of pieces that go together much like a puzzle. Jesus came, Jesus lived, Jesus died, Jesus was raised, and Jesus ascended—all of this serves as the foundation of the gospel of the Kingdom.

The first two chapters of this book emphasized the significance of the incarnation of Christ and what it means for history. The incarnation was a moment of discontinuity whereby history was forever changed. Our understanding of the past, present, and future was altered when the God who sits enthroned 'above' time entered into time to bring all of the human existence into subjection to his Lordship. In the last chapter we talked through the nature of the kingdom of God as it pertains to Christ's political rule among all nations and peoples and institutions. Our focus now is going to shift to the significance of the resurrection and what that means for the world; its meaning, of course, being something far more than what we typically assume.

Let's consider our text. 1 Corinthians 15 is a long passage *which explains the gospel as it works itself out in space and time.* The early Christian confession in the first part of the chapter sets the stage for the argument the apostle Paul will make: Christ died according to the Scriptures; was buried; and was raised according to the Scriptures (vv. 3-5). After this unprecedented event—another act of discontinuity in the world—Jesus appeared to several hundred people, including Paul himself (vv. 6-8).

After explaining the *basis* of the gospel message, he moves into the *consequence* of the gospel: Christ's resurrection and our resurrection. If Christ isn't raised, everything is basically pointless (vv. 12-19). What an incredible thing to say! If the dead aren't raised, Christ isn't raised, and if Christ isn't raised, then we're basically going to end up nihilists, so good luck. But Christ has been raised, the first fruits of those who have died (v. 20). Adam brought death; Christ brought life (vv. 21-22). Here is the crux of the argument: Christ is the first fruits (of what, exactly?); after Christ's initial first fruit, there's another resurrection: "those who are Christ's at His coming" (v. 23). After this, there's one final moment in verse 24: "Then comes the end," the end being Christ's handing over of his mediatorial Kingdom to the Father, the very Kingdom given to him at his birth (cf. Isaiah 9:6-7).

The rest of this section explains what history looks like, and it looks like Jesus putting his enemies under his feet (v. 25). During his mediatorial reign, Christ abolishes all rule and all authority and power (v. 24). King Jesus is currently reigning, and the reigning coincides with the foostooling of all enemies. The very last enemy to be conquered in history, indeed at the tail end of history's final moments, is death, which is subjected to God at the final resurrection. All of this is for the purposes of God being 'all in all' (v. 28).

That the risen Christ is the foundational principle for all of human history goes without saying. Paul is clearly intentional about making that point here in this passage. The question, nonetheless, becomes this: what is the *nature* of Christ's resurrection? How does his resurrection lead to *others* being resurrected? And what does his 'coming' mean? These questions perplex many a theologian, nevertheless, I'm going to lay some things out for you which will give more clarity on the doctrine in question.

Jesus is the first fruits of the present future. He is the beginning of the future made present. When Jesus died and was raised, the inaugural moment of the kingdom of heaven was revealed and made the now-present reality for the entire cosmos. The judicial death to atone for sin followed by the vindication of the resurrection in the middle history became the bedrock for new reality and condition: The kingdom of God is now coming to earth in a radical new way. The resurrection of Christ, quite literally, is the foundation of our faith. Furthermore, the resurrection of Christ sets the stage for the Spirit's regenerating power to be exercised in the world as history advances towards glory.

There is, therefore, much to be said about the resurrection and we would do well to pay close attention to the language Paul deploys here (and elsewhere). Paul sees the resurrection of Jesus as being the 'first fruits' of a harvest. But what harvest is he speaking of? When we enter into the world of the first century, we can conclude a few things, especially when we look at various parts of the Bible. To start, there are two harvests connected to two different festivals. During the time of the Passover (in the middle of April), barley was the first crop harvest (Exodus 9:31-32), but *there were two stages of this harvest.*[3]

First, right at the start of the harvest, there was the gleaning of the first fruits (cf. Lev. 23:4-14). A month later, there was the full harvest of ripe barley crops. The first fruits (that is, stage one) as Paul understood it, was Christ's resurrection during the Passover celebration in AD 30 (see Acts 26:23; 1 Cor. 15:20, 22-24; Col. 1:18; Heb. 12:23; Rev. 1:5; 20:4-6).

A month later was the *general* harvest of the barley crop (stage two; see Acts 24:15; 1 Cor. 15:23; Rev. 20:4, 5b, 6). The key to understanding stage two of the barley harvest is its connection to AD 70. In summation: Christ was the first fruits of the barley crop in AD 30; there was also a resurrection in AD 70 'at his coming', which is what Paul means here in 1 Corinthians 15:23. These resurrections are separated *theologically*, but they all constitute one

---

[3] I am indebted to Pastor Phil Kayser for pointing this out.

great resurrection, which is the first resurrection described in Revelation 20.

The second harvest, which is wheat grain harvest, happened 50 days later at the Pentecost celebration in early June (Deut. 16:9-12; Ruth 2:23). This goes by the name 'Feast of Weeks' in Exodus 23:16 as it was an agricultural celebration, a time of thanking God for his provision of food and sustenance. In the book of Acts, Pentecost is connected to Christ's promise of the Holy Spirit, who, in an act of resurrection life, regenerated God's people, giving them a foretaste and down payment on the future final resurrection, equipping them for dominion.

We need to keep this agricultural context in mind especially because the time between AD 30 and AD 70 was an overlapping of the ages. In AD 30, the new covenant—that is, the new heavens and new earth—began its implementation in the world. It broke through at the 'end times', which should be understood as the end of the old covenant epoch. The barley harvest, beginning with Christ's first fruits resurrection in AD 30 and concluding with the AD 70 resurrection, was the transition period as the old heavens and earth were giving way to the new heavens and new earth.

Now, I want to make sure we are clear on this, so I want to reiterate a couple things. First, Matthew 27:52 explains the powerful nature of Christ's resurrection. It was so powerful that 'graves were opened' and 'many bodies of the saints who had fallen asleep were raised', coming out of the graves 'after His resurrection', and they, too, appeared to many people. The first fruits harvest in the middle of history was such that *many* were raised with Jesus. It was quite a gleaning.

Secondly, 1 Corinthians 15:24 has a pesky Greek word parked right at the start of the sentence and it is translated as 'then', as in, "then comes the end…" The Greek word is *eita* and it refers to something that happens at a *later* time, not something that happens right away after that which was just said. The barley harvest, which happened in two stages, is described in verse 23; 'then', as in, 'at a *much later* time', there is the final wheat harvest when Christ returns to consummate history. The 'coming' is thus his 'appearing'—the *parousia* being his royal presence in the affairs of history as he brought forth judgment on Jerusalem in AD 70. The connection between Christ the firstborn from the dead and those who were raised at his AD 70 'coming' is as sure as the connection between the first part of the harvest of the barley crop and the rest of the barley crop. The rest of the barley harvest happens *shortly* after the first fruits are gleaned.

At this point in the discussion you might be wondering how we get a resurrection at AD 70. That's a good question to ask. There are several passages in the Bible which contain the Greek word *mello*, which should be translated as something that is 'about' to happen. This word carries with it the connotation of something that's happening *very* soon, not something that's happening in the distant future. I'll give you two examples.

First, Acts 17:31 says, "[B]ecause He has fixed a day in which He will [*mello*] judge the world in righteousness through a Man whom He has appointed, having furnished proof to all men by raising Him from the dead." Here Christ's resurrection is connected to imminent judgment of Israel, and Paul knows this because Daniel 12:1-3 teaches a fiery judgment followed immediately by a resurrection. In Daniel 12:2, 'many' are raised, *but not everyone*, and this is because the first century barley harvest is *one* of the resurrections, the wheat harvest at the end of history is the *other* resurrection.

Second, there are numerous 'imminent' judgment passages that describe what Acts 17:31

describes, and they, too, use the same Greek word *mello*. They are:

- Acts 24:15 (where Paul describes to Felix the coming resurrection that would happen in AD 70); he also describes it again in Acts 24:25.
- Romans 8:18 – "For I consider that the sufferings of this present time are not worthy to be compared with the glory that is to be revealed to us." Paul is saying that there is glory which is 'about' to be revealed, as in, *imminently*.
- 2 Timothy 4:1 is another passage. Paul encourages Timothy not to worry because Christ is about to judge the living and the dead, which is another reference to AD 70. AD 70, let the reader understand, is a foretaste of the judgment at the end of history.

Another New Testament passage will suffice to prove the point (see 1 Thess. 4:13-18). The Thessalonian Christians were concerned about these things. Paul was to die before AD 70 (and he did); he knew he would be raised at AD 70. But there was a slight problem: people survived AD 70 and were still alive. *What about them?* Verse 17 says, "Then we who are alive and remain will be caught up together with them in the clouds to meet the Lord in the air, and so we shall always be with the Lord." The word "then" here is the same word found in 1

Corinthians 15:23. Here Paul comforts them by saying that those who are alive 'after' the AD 70 resurrection will be good to go for the wheat harvest. *If you miss the barley harvest resurrection, hang tight, you'll catch the next harvest.*[4]

To illustrate the harvest distinctions, one only needs to look at the book of Ruth, which illustrates Christ the ultimate kinsman redeemer. Revelation puts the marriage supper of the lamb at AD 70 because when Ruth comes to Bethlehem, we are told in Ruth 1:22 that it is the beginning of the barley harvest. By the end of the barley harvest, Ruth is betrothed and married (Ruth 3:15-18). This is all done at the barley harvest, not the wheat harvest. This is the *beginning* of the mediatorial kingdom of Christ on earth, not the end. We are 'married' to Christ and we 'reign' with him, which is what Revelation 20 talks about.

Look at Revelation 20:1-6.

Then I saw an angel coming down from heaven, holding the key of the abyss and a great chain in his

---

[4] I see 1 Thessalonians 4:13-18 matching 1 Corinthians 15:23-24 perfectly. There is Christ's AD 30 "first fruits" of the barley harvest resurrection, AD 70's royal presence of Christ for judgment and resurrection as the rest of the barley resurrection, and "then" [after a long time, and thus not immediate] the final wheat harvest resurrection at the end of time (cf. 1 Thess. 4:17 with 1 Cor. 15:24).

hand. And he laid hold of the dragon, the serpent of old, who is the devil and Satan, and bound him for a thousand years; and he threw him into the abyss, and shut it and sealed it over him, so that he would not deceive the nations any longer, until the thousand years were completed; after these things he must be released for a short time. Then I saw thrones, and they sat on them, and judgment was given to them. And I saw the souls of those who had been beheaded because of their testimony of Jesus and because of the word of God, and those who had not worshiped the beast or his image, and had not received the mark on their forehead and on their hand; and they came to life and reigned with Christ for a thousand years. The rest of the dead did not come to life until the thousand years were completed. This is the first resurrection. Blessed and holy is the one who has a part in the first resurrection; over these the second death has no power, but they will be priests of God and of Christ and will reign with Him for a thousand years.

Revelation is primarily about first century events, which is why the Bible speaks the way it does about the resurrections. Those who endured the beast's tribulation, staying faithful to the end, they were raised in resurrection glory in AD 70. The 'rest', however, didn't 'come to life'—they had to wait until the wheat harvest after the millennial reign of Christ. The martyrs 'reign' as Christ 'reigns'; the rest of us in Christ 'reign' here on the earth awaiting the wheat harvest when history is consummated after Christ's enemies are defeated.

To give you a little historical context, look at what Josephus says in his book, *The Wars of the Jews*. "[O]n the twenty-first day of the month Artemisius [Jyar], a certain prodigious and incredible phenomenon appeared; I suppose the account of it would seem to be a fable, were it not related by those that saw it, and were not the events that followed it of so considerable a nature as to deserve such signals; for, before sunsetting, chariots and troops of soldiers in their armor were seen running about among the clouds, and surrounding of cities."[5] Just as Revelation 19:11-14 describes, *Jesus leads his resurrected warrior-martyrs into victory.* The Roman historian Tacitus further elucidates the event: "In the sky appeared a vision of armies in conflict, of glittering armour."[6] Christ had his martyrs join him in the battle and several saw it take place.

As we wrap this chapter up, I want to shift gears for a moment and bring it all together for us. Much

---

[5] Flavius Josephus and William Whiston, The Works of Josephus: Complete and Unabridged (Peabody: Hendrickson, 1987), 742.
[6] Tacitus, *Histories*, Book 5, v. 13.

of the debate surrounding AD 70 and so forth can be easily solved when we see the link between what Jesus said about his own body, and what he said about the temple in Jerusalem. It is clear from his remarks about the corruption of the temple and his overall contention with the temple—in places like Matthew 12:6 ('But I say to you that something greater than the temple is here') and John 2:19 ('Destroy this temple, and in three days I will raise it up')—that this was one of the main issues surrounding his ministry. The ministry of Christ, fueled by a self-conscious understanding of his role in bringing about the Kingdom, led to a massive confrontation with Jewish leaders and their beloved temple.

Quite literally, Jesus—the true temple of God, the place where heaven and earth perfectly meet— had brought the *future* glory of the temple of the people of God to the earth, and *there was no room in Jerusalem for the both of them.* The temple in the old covenant age was made as a copy of the heavenly temple where God dwells (cf. Heb. 8:5; 9:24). As we know, God does not dwell in temples made by human hands, at least not in the fullest possible way (2 Chron. 6:18; cf. Acts 17:24). Therefore, Jesus came as the tabernacle-temple (Jn. 1:14) to bring the future to the present (now past) in order to unleash the new covenant blessings of a new heaven and new earth. Jesus the temple upending the real temple in Jerusalem in order establish the people of God as a temple where Christ's Spirit dwells. This people-of-God-temple expands and contracts, growing slowly through time in an ever-increasing way as the gospel smashes idols and takes men captive to the grace of God. (More on this theology in the next chapter.)

The place where heaven and earth touch could never be a temple made of brick and stone. No, it needed to be a temple made of glory and righteousness. In order for a new temple to be constructed, it needed *living* stones. And how does God get living stones? He regenerates them. How does he regenerate them? He brings the future into the present in a collision of astronomical proportions—what we call, the death and resurrection of Christ Jesus.

The resurrection of Christ was the first fruits of the present future. The paradigm looks like this: future glory stepped into the present to shape the future. The glories of resurrection life—the type of life that Jesus Christ enjoys right now—is brought into human history with Holy Spirit power for the renewal of the cosmos. This new covenant paradigm is now the working condition and reality of the rest of history. We do not function as humanists with reincarnation and materialistic determinism. We function in this world as ambassadors of Christ with whole life insurance, not term life insurance: we have the deposit of resurrection hope in the here and now. It is the *present* future. Christ in his resurrection has injected into history a bright hope of victory and conquest.

Which means we must enjoy this victory. We must not live as people without resurrection hope. We *have hope.* Why? Because Christ was born, Christ lived, Christ died, Christ was raised, and Christ is enthroned. The process of the harvest has already begun. It's our job to reap the harvest, after all, the harvest is absolutely plentiful. The workers, however, are few.

4
ALL THINGS NEW

And He who sits on the throne said,
"Behold, I am making all things new."
Revelation 21:5

There are innumerable questions we can ask when it comes to Eschatology, and this is because there are innumerable questions we could ask about the Bible in general. Why did God create the universe? Where was God before everything was made? Why didn't Jesus come the moment Adam sinned? What about the Christmas story—why does it matter that Mary was a virgin? Questions abound because to a large degree, we struggle to take the revelation of God and grasp it with our inept, sin-tainted faculties. This is, of course, because sin does more than affect our physical world; it affects the metaphysical as well.

We cannot and must not, therefore, go the existentialist route, adopting a post-enlightenment rationalism which pits the elevated mind against God. We also cannot and must not go the deistic route either and posit a god whose rather unconcerned with our minds as it is. And yet, we know from Scripture that the biblical God is not the author of confusion (1 Cor. 14:33). God is not interested in revealing himself in an unintelligible fashion. God is Creator, and God is the grand Speaker—he and only he has the microphone on the stage of the universe.

In light of this, there is, out of all the innumerable questions, an important one I'd like to ask and it has everything to do with what we've been discussing in this book: *Why does it matter that the Second Person of the Trinity took on flesh?* Why is it significant, indeed crucial to the Christian faith, that Jesus entered into space and time, shaking up the cosmos, and making the revelation and presence of God more—if we can call it this—*palpable*? The answer, I suggest, is this: Because God is faithful to his creation. He is committed to that which he intends to orchestrate for history. The Creator is faithful and loyal to that which he has created and ordained. God-in-the-flesh came as a covenantally loyal God to bring about a new creation. But what exactly does that mean?

The last couple of chapters to the book of Revelation built on Old Testament themes from places like Daniel, Jeremiah, and Ezekiel, however, one key passage that John the Revelator pulls from is the last two chapters of Isaiah. When John catches a glimpse of what's taking place in heaven—and there is much action occurring—he's getting a glimpse of the new covenant (what we call the new heavens and new earth) and how it intends on transforming the world. What's taking place in heaven is in preparation for the earth. Or rather, what's decreed in heaven comes about on the earth. John alludes to Isaiah 65:17, which reads, "For behold, I create new heavens and a new earth; and the former things will not be remembered or come to mind." He also pulls from Isaiah 66:22, which expresses a similar sentiment: "'For just as the new heavens and the new earth which I make will endure before me' declares the LORD, 'So your offspring and your name will endure'."

It's been aptly stated that in Revelation 21:5, Jesus did *not* say, 'Behold, I am making *all new things*', rather, he said, "Behold, I am making all things *new.*" This is, of course, a fine thing to say, but it doesn't really explain what it is Jesus is getting at. What are the things? What is new about them?

This being the case, I will fill you in on my understanding of the verse, and I will be appealing to other Scriptures in the process.

When it comes to eschatology, we need to keep in mind the language of 'continuity' and 'discontinuity'. If you recall from chapter one, we established the fact that there were two remarkable events which were extraordinary discontinuities that could only come from Someone 'above' time intervening in the continuous affairs of a sinful world. Because the Triune God chose to act, these two moments of discontinuity were the incarnation and the resurrection. The virgin-birth was a discontinuity. The *death* of Christ was continuous with the sinful status quo (men simply die). The resurrection, however, was another discontinuity— the one that fulfills what the first discontinuity had set out to do. What men had done to disintegrate themselves from God in history, Christ had come to capture these people and reintegrate them back into covenant.

As we covered in the previous chapter, the resurrection was the future breaking into the present in order to alter the course of human history, moving it from death to life, from wrath to grace, from darkness to light. Because of the nature of this powerful resurrection, we are able to see what it is the New Testament is trying to teach us with regard to the new creation. In Paul's language, the individual has been transformed into a new creation (2 Cor. 5:17). In John's language, quoting Christ himself, the cosmos is being transformed into a new creation (Rev. 21:5; Is. 65:17). In Jesus' own words, echoing Isaiah 35, the great eschatological fulfillment of Sabbath and new creation is now present in his own ministry (cf. Matthew 11). The Spirit's regenerating power that burst forth on the scene of history that Sunday morning was the defining moment of discontinuity *when the new creation would become the new continuity.* What had been disintegrated is now reintegrated into a new humanity. Quite literally, the resurrection of Christ became a ripple effect which spread across the universe. What heaven has declared Christ is now implementing. How do we know this?

When Christ was raised, the disciples were able to recognize him, but only after Jesus disclosed himself to them. The disciples on the road to Emmaus didn't know it was him (Luke 24:13-49), yet Thomas was able recognize him and feel the hole the Roman nails had left behind in his hands (John 20:19-29). What we should conclude from this is both continuity and discontinuity: Jesus still had the visible wounds, yet he was alive in a glorified body. Interestingly enough, whoever it was that met the risen Christ was also met with *astonishment*. The new had transformed the old, or, perhaps more aptly stated, the eschatologically 'new' creates a *new* continuity, never fully annihilating and eradicating the old, as if it were something to throw away in a cosmic trash can, but rather, taking the old and creating it new.

When Jesus says, 'Behold, I am making all things new,' he is not suggesting that another creation is going to come about after this one is destroyed. (Which is why 2 Peter 3 is most emphatically *not* talking about a literal fire blowing up the planet.) How do we know this? 1 Corinthians 15:53 reads, with my emphasis, "For *this* perishable must put on the imperishable, and *this* mortal must put on immortality." The resurrected Christ was the *crucified* Christ—and not another person coming to replace the other. As an artist, God is faithful to his creation, and thus he spends his time shaping and reshaping, molding and remolding, taking that which was originally 'good', which has been, sadly, continuously marked by sin and injustice, and making it *creatio nova*—a (re)new(ed) creation. As time progressed, the old order was marked by aging and entropic senescence—a deterioration. Life moves towards death, young moves toward old. The way *out* of this is the risen Christ 'making all things new'.

To ensure I'm being understood, let me say this another way. The resurrection of Jesus of Nazareth stands in the middle of human history as the fulcrum on which the world pivots. This great eschatological moment was the future breaking into the present in order to re-shape the future for glory. The new creation—what we call the kingdom of heaven— was not and is not an altogether completely different thing, rather, it's *the remaking of the old into new.* 'This' mortal takes on immortality. 'This' perishable takes on imperishable. When humanity sows sin, it reaps death. When God sows righteousness, he reaps eternal life. When the new creation entered into history through the death and resurrection of Christ, the world was set on a different path, one of righteousness, justice, and peace. The discontinuity of resurrection brought forth a new continuity, a new reality and condition, the kingdom of heaven on the earth.

As we consider the theology I just outlined, it is important to note that this process of all things being made 'new' involves human vocation and activity. Adam and Eve were created to be vice-regents, and while sin hampered this divine calling, Jesus the Second Adam has brought us into himself and thus back into this calling. The vocation I'm speaking of is tied to the doctrine of the *imago Dei*: the image of God. As image bearers, our vocation is to reflect the glory of God, which is another way of saying, we must obey God and see to it that all areas of life know its obligation to do the same.

So, then, what is the role of humans? The Christian answer differs from the humanist answer. For the humanist, the role of humanity is the ever-increasing process of self-actualization. We must learn to 'be who we are' and express ourselves despite that which may or may not be in *vogue*. Mantras such as 'you do you' and 'speak your truth' are the relativist's attempt at self-maturation. It's their sanctification program. With God out of the picture, all that's left is *you* and only *you* can be *you*. No one can say anything different. Sanctification, in this manner of thinking, is entirely monergistic, the only contributing factor is *self*.

To the contrary, Christian doctrine believes that the role of humans is to speak how God speaks and act how God acts. Our vocation is one of mimicry:

do as *Abba* does. In all lawful areas of government (self, family, church, and civil), we are to bring that area into obedience and subjection through service and righteousness. At the heart of it is the recognition that the vision of God from Genesis to Revelation is the vision of Leviticus 26:11-12 which reads, "Moreover, I will make My dwelling among you, and My soul will not reject you. I will also walk among you and be your God, and you shall by My people." [If you take a quick look at Revelation 21:3, you'll see the very same language.]

In other words, our calling is priestly, prophetic, and kingly as we serve the living God. Adam was placed in the Garden-Temple, yet he disobeyed. God, desiring to dwell with his people, entered into the tabernacle and temple, yet Israel, God's son, disobeyed. Two sons, two acts of disobedience. Jesus Christ, carrying forward the very same vision, became the cornerstone of the new temple, the stone the builders had rejected. Christ's activity thus became the foundation of a new temple, the city-temple of God, which is the hallmark of the new heavens and new earth. That temple is God's people. Christ taking on humanity after humanity had traded in its image bearing responsibility was the great reclamation and work of the kingdom of God.

The role of humanity, then, if we want to be true to Christmas, is to exercise the prophetic, priestly, and kingly responsibilities that we now possess as members of Christ. We are to shed light in the dark world as prophets who herald the truth about God and reality. As priests, we are to steward and care for the world, not least the *people* in the world, by providing assistance, healing, and nurture to those who are hurting. As kings, we are responsible to manage God's covenant institutions by faithfully discharging our kingly calling to administrative guardianship of the covenant blessings God has given us. This means that we have answers for the realm of money and healthcare and education. We have solutions to the problems that perplex society in places like politics and criminology. Our task is the healing of the nations, and the saving balm of the justice and mercy of Christ is the only true and lasting balm.

As image bearers we are given this great responsibility, but we must understand the eschatological context in which it moves and has its being. When Adam and Eve sinned, their ethical rebellion brought forth an eschatological context which separated the fulness of God's presence from them. Quite literally, God had conceded space for

Adam and Eve to live, the creation itself being subjected to futility. Think of it this way: God does not, in an absolute sense, manifest his glory and omnipresence in the created order, otherwise, there would be no creation. Heaven itself can't contain him (2 Chron. 6:18). The condition Adam and Eve have left the world in after their rebellion was not fit for God's presence, nor could it have been had God chosen to do so. You might say, God had veiled his glory in order to execute his plan for redemption. He held himself back. This veiling was a sort of remoteness and spatial distance necessary to enter into creation in order to redeem it.

So, the space of creation was a concession given to man in order for man to exercise subordinating dominion under the authority of God. The eschatological context we must keep in mind is the fact that while God had distanced himself in terms of the fullness of his presence after Adam had sinned, the goal of the created order was and still is the presence of the fulness of God. The temple language from Genesis to Revelation, picked up in Leviticus 26 and Revelation 21, is the way God has chosen to speak about his dwelling with man. The whole of creation is the temple of God, the house of God, the place where God's Sabbath rest must be located.

Made in God's image, man participates—to some degree—in this glory and rest because, in spite of his sin, man has breath in his lungs and a place to lay his weary, sin-stricken head. This is grace.

The eschatological context, then, becomes the great unification of heaven and earth, the remarkable bridging of the gaps between God and man, and all of this is done through the gospel of the Kingdom. When God broke in that starry night when Christ was born, that was the moment when creation began to lose its space 'outside' of God, and becomes, by God's grace, a place where God comes to dwell. There is a mutual indwelling—the world in God's presence, God's presence in the world—where humanity is made new, and creation is made new.

Atheism posits a formula where 'god' is rolled up into man's collective reason—man becomes a god. Pantheism and paganism posits a formula where nature is rolled up into 'god'. To the contrary, Christian teaching says that there is a mutual indwelling where the created order remains distinguishable from God. God is in the world, and the two are still covenantally discernible. We will always know for eternity that which is God and that which is *not* God.

The point of this eschatological context, as I see it, has everything to do with what it is we are laboring for. We have this great task of the healing of the nations. But we have this task set within the context of God's great plan to dwell with man. Because of the resurrection of Christ, this grand reversal of sin and spatial distance is being undone. 'All things new' means the transformation of the world in order to make it a space for the fulness of God's presence to dwell. That's the vision of Isaiah, and that's the vision of Revelation. This new heavens and new earth, the new temple-people-of-God, is the means by which this is all accomplished. Our labor is not in vain because our labor serves this great plan.

And what I find absolutely thrilling is the fact that the in-breaking of the Kingdom the moment Christ was born—the Kingdom being legally set forth in his death and resurrection—became the basis for God's plan to reverse the curse and create a world where sin is dismissed and holiness runs rampant. From thenceforth God has determined to undermine the forces of evil, putting a progressive end to problem of sin and injustice.

As I see it, we are working towards this goal and it will be self-consciously realized as history progresses. As the gospel goes forth, and as the knowledge of the glory of the LORD covers the earth as the waters cover the sea, men will self-consciously see that this is where history is headed, and *they will know*. We are still in the early church. It is still very early in the eschatological plan of redemption. But we are working towards this moment when Christ comes in a history-ending way to bring his plan to completion.

Which means we should be working to live longer, as Isaiah intimates (Is. 65:20). The current humanist-driven, reductionistic allopathy we call 'conventional medicine' isn't going to get the job done. Living well beyond 100 years should be a goal, but it isn't going to happen with the humanists in control of food and health—which isn't food and it isn't health.

We should be seeking worldwide peace but not through the military industrial complex of American foreign policy, which is a recapitulation of the *pax Romana* (the peace of Rome) of the Caesars. Peace can only come from the Prince of Peace, and only when the gospel is tasted and seen.

We should be working towards technological development to reverse the curse. These are good and righteous things. However, we must do so within this eschatological context. To try and rebuild the Tower of Babel when the Temple of the living God (the Church) is here is a fruitless endeavor. *Our aim is the kingdom of God made palpable and present in the affairs of mankind—his heart, his mind, and his institutions.*

'All things new' is our aim. The resurrection of Christ is our confidence. We have what we need, so we must, then, if we are to have an eschatological Christmas, get to work to roll back the entropy and decadence and see to it that God is welcome to dwell with us. Grab a sword, grab a shovel, and *build.*

EPILOGUE

*The conclusion, when all has been heard, is: fear God
and keep His commandments, because this applies to every
person. For God will bring every act to judgment,
everything which is hidden, whether it is good or evil.*
Ecclesiastes 12:13-14

God is the self-contained, absolute personality.
Meaning, unlike other views of God in pagan or
religious contexts, the biblical God is self-existent
and self-sufficient ('self-contained'). He does not
need something to fill him, for the fulness of deity
dwells in him and in nothing else. God is a
personality in that he speaks and acts and thinks. He
judges and moves about in and out of history. The
Triune God is never at the behest of someone or
something else, nor does he have some portion of
his intellect in need of filling. God doesn't need
Google.

I have tried, in this short book, to provide some
contours as it pertains to the relationship between
eschatology and Christmas. Not that Christmas is

only about the advent of Christ—far be it! Christmas is simply the *beginning*, the starting point of God's great plan to bring all things into subjection to himself. Being the absolute personality that he is, God does not 'need' mankind or creation to be brought forth into glory because he's missing something. God does all of this because he's just that gracious. He is decidedly *for* his people and his creation. He loves us enough to keep us from destroying and disintegrating ourselves and he proved it that Christmas day. The remarkable thing about Christmas is the fact that it demonstrates God's love in a way never seen before. The God of Abraham, Isaac, and Jacob—the God of the covenant—came to us, he is *Immanuel.*

So, what shall we do? How shall we live? Serve him entirely. Fear him and keep his commandments. God is the Judge, he sees all, and nothing is hidden. That's why it's called *light.* Whether good or evil, he sees, and that's supposed to comfort us. May you be comforted in your celebration of Christmas.

ABOUT THE AUTHOR

Dr. Jason Garwood has spent his career seeking to both understand and apply the Biblical worldview to every single area of life. His aim is to help pastors and churches to be better equipped to engage in the Great Commission by teaching Christians how to find their individual purpose in the Kingdom of God and learn how to identify and respond to cultural idols.

He is currently the teaching pastor at Cross & Crown Church in Northern Virginia:
- Cross & Crown was planted in 2017 with a vision and mission to equip men, women, and children to press the crown rights of King Jesus into every area of life;
- Cross & Crown is a house-church movement seeking to establish other house churches across the world; and
- Cross & Crown is laboring to promote liberty and justice by local activism and involvement in the community.

He is a writer and activist:
- Jason is the author of four books, including *Reconstructing the Heart* and *The Politics of Humanism*;

- He has written articles for various outlets and blogs at jasongarwood.com; and
- He has preached and lectured internationally on a variety of subjects, exposing the underling errors and problems with anti-biblical worldviews such as: government education, the drug war, the police state, humanist philosophy, and vaccines;
- You can find him at college campuses, high schools, and political meetings seeding the gospel of the Kingdom of Jesus Christ.

Most importantly, Jason is a devoted husband and father:
- He has been married to his wife, Mary, for 13 years;
- They have three children;
- He makes his home in Warrenton, Virginia.